The Call of the Stars

Five Wonderful Stories of People Looking to the Heavens

Nury Vittachi

Illustrations by Step Cheung

Contents

THE BOY WHO DECODED THE DANCE OF THE STARS

JEREMIAH LOVED THE STARS, but he was too young and too poor to be an astronomer.

He was the child of a poor family in the UK a long time ago, in the early 1600s.

While other children played, Jeremiah Horrocks saved his energy until the evening, when he could watch the stars starting to twinkle in the deep blue evening sky.

The way they "danced" in different directions and at different speeds as they moved across the sky might be a code which could reveal secrets about the galaxy, he believed.

When he was 13, Jeremiah, who was very bright, went to university, where he learned from astronomers and used their telescopes.

But before he could graduate, his family ran out of money, and he had to return home.

He was sad at first, but then had an idea. His father worked for a watchmaker. He knew how to do three things: shape metal, form circles of glass, and make very precise instruments.

These were the exact three things you needed to make a telescope!

By the time he was in his late teens, Jeremiah was working to earn money during the day (he was a trainee church pastor and a private tutor), and he was working with his family members to make his own telescope during the evenings.

One day, when he was 19 or 20, his observations of star movements gave him an idea.

Although the sun appeared to rise in the East and move across the sky to the West, he was convinced that it was actually a huge distance away, much further than the moon, millions of miles or kilometers from the Earth.

And he realized that he could actually prove it, if he was right about the way the lights in the heavens continued on their dances.

On one particular day soon, according to his calculations, the planet Venus would come in between the Earth and the Sun, far out in space.

This would be proof that the sun was not in the sky, as it seemed to be, but an unimaginably large distance away.

That day, he got up at sunrise. He knew he should not look directly at the sun, so he set up his telescope to project an image of the sun onto a piece of paper.

And he watched and waited.

It was disappointing. He saw nothing interesting, although he watched for hours.

In the afternoon, clouds appeared and both he and the sky become gloomy.

But then, at 3.15 p.m., the clouds parted.

His telescope showed an amazing sight! He could see a dot crossing a circle.

He knew exactly what it was. In his head, he could visualize a huge planet as a small, round, dark silhouette passing in front of a massive burning fire-golden orb.

This proved the sun was tens of millions of miles away, further than Venus.

He wrote down his findings — partly in poetry — and then sent them to London, to the Royal Society, the world's top science organization.

But this story has a sad ending. In those days, medical science was undeveloped, and people who got sick often died. Jeremiah Horrocks became ill and died at the age of 22.

Years later, people discovered his letter and realized that he was one of the greatest scientists in the country, even though he was just a child when he did most of his work.

In 2012, scientists using special hi-tech cameras in space watched, for the first time, Venus crossing in front of the sun in clear detail (and you can watch it yourself on the Internet: look up "transit of Venus").

Humanity finally saw what young Jeremiah had seen in his head 400 years earlier!

THE POET-SCIENTIST WHO DETECTED AN EARTHQUAKE

THE FUTURE LOOKED BAD for a boy call Zhang Heng, aged ten. The family did not have much money, and then his father died.

Even worse, Heng was only really good at one thing: writing poems. What use was that? He was a bookworm, not like his grandfather, who was an army commander. The family struggled to survive.

When Zhang Heng was 16 years old, in the year AD 95, he left his hometown of Xi'e in Nanyang, Henan province, China, and started to travel to the big city nearby, to see if he could get a job.

On his way, he stopped at a hot spring and wrote a poem about it.

Then he arrived in town. The good thing was that people in power in the big city remembered his family's past achievements, and agreed to see him. It turned out that they were in need of writers — so he was given a post as a Master of Documents for the officials in the government.

Being a bookworm can be a good thing.

His poem about the hot springs became famous.

One day, when Zhang Heng was 30, he stared up at the night sky.

That's the sort of thing most poets do. But instead of just writing a poem about it, he started to notice things.

The moon had two sides, a light side that we always saw, and a dark side that was always invisible. And he realized that it was the sun shining on the moon that caused it to seem to change shape. In reality, it didn't change shape at all.

He noticed constellations of stars, and separate stars which seemed to be on their own. He decided to make a star map.

These sort of activities seem normal to us today — but in those days, almost 2,000 years ago — he was one of the first of his kind.

And remember, he had no telescope or binoculars, or even glasses. He just waited until night and then gazed up at the sky.

Zhang Heng catalogued more than 2,500 stars, and his observations made him one of the first great astronomers.

Some of his star maps still survive today. His work was continued almost 2,000 years later by a young woman, as we will learn later in this book, in the story which begins on page 15.

Having fallen in love with science, Zhang Heng did other things too. He is said to have invented a seismometer, which is a machine to detect earthquakes.

One day, the device trembled, and indicated a particular direction.

"Look," he told the other nobles. "It says there has just been an earthquake to the northwest."

But had that really happened? The matter was discussed, and citizens agreed that none of them had felt any kind of tremor.

Just when everyone was starting to think he might be a bit crazy, a rider arrived, breathless, saying that there had been an earthquake 400 kilometers to the northwest.

There is not enough information about his device to know for sure how it works, but there is enough detail given about it to intrigue people, so many inventors have tried to recreate his seismograph machine, none successfully yet.

Zhang Heng soon became a powerful nobleman, and he attracted enemies who said bad things about him to the emperor.

He responded in a way that only he could. To set the record straight, he wrote a poem.

THE FARM BOY WHO SAW THE GALAXIES FLYING AWAY

GETTING UP EARLY CAN BE HARD. But what if you worked on a farm, and had to get up so early that it was always still dark?

A boy called Vesto Slipher had to do that. But he didn't mind. He loved the night sky — and began to feel that his future might be up there, in the stars. It was 1875 in the USA, and the night sky was huge and black and glittery, with no airplanes or pollution. And that meant that you could see all sorts of things above you: not just the moon and stars, but the twinkling Milky Way and magical distant star clouds.

It was a good thing he had an interest, because he was one of 11 children, so he didn't get much attention from his parents.

He worked hard and studied hard, and soon got into a university to study astronomy and engineering.

In 1901, his professor asked a rich and famous local astronomer, Percival Lowell, to give the hardworking young man a job at his observatory.

Lowell was a busy man, and so he was not very enthusiastic about managing a youngster. But he said he would give a "short-term" contract to the young man, so that the lad could get a little work experience.

But the pair turned into a good team. Slipher was quiet and shy, so he was unobtrusive — which means he preferred to work quietly in the background. But he also worked very hard, producing a lot of interesting results.

In contrast, Lowell was flamboyant and loved to be the center of attention, explaining to the press and public what the results that Slipher collected meant.

The "short-term" contract turned into a partnership that lasted more than 50 years!

One day, Lowell told Vesto Slipher to do a difficult job: to take pictures of distant star clouds, or nebulae (huge clouds of space dust), and analyze the light that come from them, using equipment to break the white light into a rainbow of colors,

STEP C.

and recording the differences, if any.

Vesto spent weeks working on this, and noticed something odd — some star clouds had a blue blur, and others had a red blur.

He knew from his science studies what this meant. Things looked blue if they were speeding towards you and red if they were speeding away from you.

He reported to his boss that the distant star clouds were actually galaxies moving at high speed — up to 1,000 kilometers a second, faster than the fastest jet aircraft!

This was the moment when humanity discovered the truth about the universe. It looked still — but it was really a hyper-active place, with everything moving.

And what's more, we were in just one galaxy, out of many hundreds of thousands of galaxies, all zooming around at unimaginable speeds.

The finding eventually led to scientists making lots of other discoveries, such as the fact that the universe was expanding, that it was very old, and that it may have come from a Big Bang, and so on.

But all this came from the simplest of beginnings: a boy on a farm, looking up at the night sky and wanting to unravel the mysteries above him.

THE GIRL WHO NAMED THE STARS IN THE SKY

HAVE YOU EVER LOOKED up at the sky on a dark night and seen stars coming into focus over your head?

If you are away from city lights, sometimes you can see hundreds, or even thousands of stars. It's an entrancing sight.

Now, there was one particular child who had this experience, and made an amazing decision early in her life: she wanted to identify every single star in the sky, however long it took!

But there was one problem. She was a girl.

In those days, the late 1800s, many jobs were reserved for men only — particularly jobs which involved mathematics and science.

So this young lady, whose name was Annie Jump Cannon, joined an observatory — a building with telescopes with which people studied the night sky.

Because she was a girl, the men told her that she could never be promoted above the rank of "assistant". The "proper" jobs were reserved for men. This seems shocking to us now, but it was normal in those days, not just in the USA where she lived, but around the world.

The work turned out to be really hard. She needed to create a system that divided the entire night sky into sections, and find a way to write down the location of each pinpoint of light.

She also needed to write down what sort of light it was. Have you noticed, some stars are bright, while others are dim? Also, some seem bigger than others. And some stars twinkle while others shine in a steady way. Some are slightly blue or a little bit red or have a yellow tint to them.

Annie Jump Cannon needed a system that would cover all eventualities.

The work was quite tedious, which meant that it needed careful, repetitive work. Most of the men did not have the patience to do this, so Annie and some of the other women ended up doing most of it.

She was so good at it that she became well known among the world community of astronomers.

After a few years, the stargazing community realized that Annie had identified an astonishing 500,000 stars — more than all the male astronomers in the world put together, in all of history!

What's more, her way of describing each star, known as her "stellar classification system", was considered so useful that astronomers all over the world, including in Europe and Asia, adopted it.

And that little girl who loved looking at the stars is remembered as the queen of the night sky.

THE BOY WHO UNDERSTOOD EINSTEIN

GROWN-UPS RARELY GET excited about things, but sometimes something in the news gets their attention.

An eight-year-old boy called Michio was intrigued when all the grown-ups started talking about a man called Albert Einstein who had just died.

This was 1955, and radio reports said Einstein discovered lots of things about the universe that were so complicated that most people would never be able to understand them.

Stars and planets had "gravity wells" around them, and if you travelled at the speed of light to another galaxy and came back, time would have passed for you at a different rate compared to your family members who stayed at your home planet.

It was all eye-widening stuff!

Michio Kaku, a boy born to an American family with Japanese roots, learned that the media called the man who had just died "a scientist", but Einstein preferred to call himself "an artist".

The white-haired genius worked more like an author, sitting at his desk thinking and writing. He didn't wear white coats and do experiments in labs with beakers and Bunsen burners.

Puzzled, Michio Kaku decided to study physics himself.

It was tricky at first, but he found it fun — which often happens when you have a strong personal interest in a tough subject.

By the time Michio was a teenager, he was doing remarkable things. His contribution to a display of school projects was a particle accelerator.

Of course, it wasn't such a fancy one as the huge one in Europe (27 kilometers long) known as CERN, which makes lots of headlines in the newspapers.

But it did actually work.

Even most of the grown-ups visiting the school had no idea what a particle accelerator was, so Michio had to explain to them that if you used a machine to slam invisibly small particles together, they would sometimes crack open and you could get interesting information about the basic elements which make up the universe.

The fact that a teenager was trying to detect or create anti-matter, stuff that most other children would only encounter in comic books, got people's attention.

A working scientist took an interest in Michio and helped him get into good science universities, where he became a star student.

But it wasn't until Michio became an adult working as a science professor himself that he found the perfect job for himself.

Instead of working in labs, he decided that he would contribute more to society as an explainer of science.

And that's what he became. Today he is an author who writes books and hosts television shows teaching people about the wonders of physics.

And yes, even today, one of the things he is often called on to do is to explain the discoveries of Einstein — and he can do it in such a way that even eight-year-olds can understand.

Any maybe you, dear reader, may be inspired by this page to go from learning about scientists like Michio Kaku to being one yourself — and then the circle of life will continue to turn.

KEEP READING

READING ABOUT THE LIVES of scientists and other discoverers adds to our store of knowledge, but we hope also leads us towards something much greater, which is wisdom.

This book is part of a series, which we hope you'll enjoy reading, and will spur you on to do your own scientific research.

The creators of this book wish you success in your explorations.

THE YOUNG SCIENTISTS SERIES

Book 1: SECRETS IN THE ROCKS
Five Astounding Tales of People Solving Mysteries Beneath Our Feet

Book 2: FABULOUS PHYSICS
Five Amazing Stories of People Who Solved Nature's Puzzles

Book 3: MAGICAL MATHEMATICS
Five Astonishing Stories of People Who Did Miracles with Numbers

Book 4: BREAKERS OF BARRIERS
Five Stunning Stories of People Demolishing Walls to Make History

Book 5: SCIENTIFIC PIONEERS
Five Incredible Tales of People Who Helped Develop the Scientific Method

Book 6: THE AMAZING QUANTUM
Five Awesome Stories of People Who Made a Revolution in Physics

Book 7: THE SCIENCE OF HUMANITY
Five Fascinating Stories of People Who Helped Us Understand Ourselves

Book 8: WOMEN OF DISCOVERY
Five Super Stories of Fabulous Females Who Made Scientific History

Book 9: THE INVENTOR'S SPARK
Five Marvelous Stories of People Who Helped Shape the Modern World

Book 10: ADVANCES IN ALCHEMY
Five Startling Stories of Chemistry and Biology

Book 11: THE CALL OF THE STARS
Five Wonderful Stories of People Looking to the Heavens

Book 12: MYSTERIES OF NATURE'S LAWS
Five Striking Stories of People Investigating the Deepest Puzzles of Reality

Published by

WS Education, an imprint of
World Scientific Publishing Co. Pte. Ltd.
5 Toh Tuck Link, Singapore 596224
USA office: 27 Warren Street, Suite 401-402, Hackensack, NJ 07601
UK office: 57 Shelton Street, Covent Garden, London WC2H 9HE

National Library Board, Singapore Cataloguing in Publication Data
Name(s): Vittachi, Nury, 1958– | Cheung, Step, illustrator.
Title: The call of the stars : five wonderful stories of people looking to the heavens / author, Nury Vittachi ; illustrator, Step Cheung.
Other title(s): Young scientists series ; 11.
Description: Singapore : World Scientific Publishing Co Pte Ltd, 2017.
Identifier(s): OCN 969709245 | ISBN 978-981-3221-72-7 (paperback)
Subject(s): LCSH: Astronomers--Juvenile literature. | Scientists--Juvenile literature. | Astronomy--Juvenile literature. | Science--Juvenile literature.
Classification: DDC 520.922--dc23

British Library Cataloguing-in-Publication Data
A catalogue record for this book is available from the British Library.

All royalties received will be channelled to the National Book Development Council of Singapore (NBDCS) as a gift from the author.

First published 2017
Reprinted 2018

Printed in Singapore